THE CURE

THE ANTIDOTE TO ALL
PAIN AND UNHAPPINESS

GREGORY DICKOW

The Cure: The Antidote to All Pain and Unhappiness
©2018 by Gregory Dickow Ministries.

All rights reserved.

Printed in the United States of America

For information, please write:
Gregory Dickow Ministries
P.O. Box 7000
Chicago, IL 60680

You can visit us online at:
www.gregorydickow.com

ISBN 13: 978-1-932833-32-4

First Printing, 2018

TABLE OF CONTENTS

SOMEONE HAS STOLEN OUR TENT!

Chapter One

Remember the old western mythical hero, the Lone Ranger? He was the masked crusader that fought outlaws along with his Native American sidekick, Tonto.

The story is told that the Lone Ranger and Tonto camped in the desert one night, set up their tent, and fell asleep. Some hours later, the Lone Ranger wakes his faithful friend:

"Tonto, look up at the sky and tell me what you see."

Tonto replies, "Me see millions of stars."

"What does that tell you?", asks the Lone Ranger.

Tonto ponders for a minute.

"Astronomically speaking, it tells me that there are millions of galaxies and potentially billions of planets. Astrologically, it tells me that Saturn is in Leo. Timewise, it appears to be approximately a quarter past three. Theologically, it's evident the Lord is all powerful and we are small and in need of Him.

Meteorologically, it seems we will have a beautiful day tomorrow. What it tell you, Kemo Sabe?"

The Lone Ranger is silent for a moment, then speaks:

"Tonto, you idiot! Someone has stolen our tent!"

Well I'm writing today to tell you, "Someone has stolen our tent!" What I mean is: we've complicated life so much that we have missed the most obvious things. Jesus wants you well! And He wants you full of joy! HE wants you happy. And let's not over-spiritualize how joy is spiritual and eternal, while happiness is unspiritual or temporal. Happiness was God's idea.

"Happy are the people who are in such a state; Happy are the people whose God is the Lord!" (Psalm 144:15)

I believe God uses the word: "happy" here, for a very important reason . . . He means it! Haha☺

"You shall be happy, and it shall be well with you." (Psalm 128:2)

"Happy is he who has the God of Jacob for his help, Whose hope is in the Lord his God." (Psalm 146:5)

There is no higher or deeper desire in the heart of man-kind, than happiness. It is the single most intoxicating emotion that drives every decision and pursuit in all our lives.

The tragedy of man's search is NOT that he cannot find happiness, but that he searches for it in the wrong places.

PAIN & PLEASURE

Chapter Two

Jesus was "a man of sorrows, and acquainted with grief" (Isaiah 53:3), "He has borne our griefs and carried our sorrows" (Isaiah 53:4a), He was stricken, [and] smitten by God, and afflicted" (Isaiah 53:4b), "He was pierced for our transgressions; He was crushed for our iniquities" (Isaiah 53:5a), "upon Him was the chastisement that brought us peace, and with His wounds we are healed" (Isaiah 53:5), "He was oppressed, and He was afflicted" (Isaiah 53:7), because "the Lord has laid on Him the iniquity of us all" (Isaiah 53:6b).

This scripture is so vital to our lives, because we all know what it's like to suffer some sort of pain. And Jesus paid for it all! And if you think about the world today, we need this healing more than ever!

Pain and unhappiness are universal. Just look around . . .

Besides the millions and millions of people suffering from chronic physical illness, anxiety, and depressive disorders, there are close to 10 million people just in the

US with eating disorders. Over 22 million are dealing with substance abuse. Heroin addiction among 18–25 year olds has doubled in the past 10 years.

- 40,000,000 in America suffer from anxiety.

- 350,000,000 worldwide suffer from depression.

- Over 60,000,000 people suffer from a mental health disorder in America. Almost 1 out of 4 adults.

- Almost 1 million people commit suicide each year around the world.

- **The COSTS alone for these things have put our nation and so many others in financial crisis. Consider these stats:** Violence costs $1.7 trillion per year in America (10 percent of GDP). This includes the prevention, police involvement, and treatment, etc.

- At least 1 in 4 women experience domestic violence.

- Youth-violent deaths in America occur 10 times more than other industrialized nations.

I don't share these statistics to depress anyone (Although I'm starting to get depressed by these myself!)

But, I'm simply sharing a few of these to validate and quantify what most of us already know: People are hurting and in need of a Healer! "Health and happiness" isn't a catch phrase. It's the number ONE thing we do everything to obtain.

And so THE SEARCH FOR HAPPINESS and freedom from pain is the sum of all human desire.

Great scientist and philosopher, Blaise Pascal said, *"All men seek happiness. This is the motive of every action of every man, even of those who hang themselves."*

This quote is very powerful to me, because when I was young, I strongly considered suicide. And in fact, one of my closest friends actually did. It devastated me. I'm not the only one. We've all been affected by someone who has taken their life or come narrowly close to that point in life.

If this issue doesn't affect you, thank God! But read on and maybe give a copy of this book to a teenager or a veteran; or give to anyone else who wants to be free from pain and full of joy.

Suicide among teens is at an all-time high. Among girls 15–19 years old, it doubled from 2007 to 2015; and it grew 30 percent among boys.

Approximately 20 veterans take their own lives in America EVERY DAY. In fact, in 2012, tragically, more veterans succumbed to suicide than were killed in combat in the war in Iraq.

This has to change!

I want them well! More importantly, God wants them well. And He wants you and me well. And He has *the cure*.

But think about it—why does someone even contemplate this thought of suicide? Why do we seek the things that make us laugh and the things that make us stop hurting? Why does someone get addicted to anything? What really is at the core of our deepest needs? Simply stated, we are all seeking two things: to alleviate pain or obtain pleasure. And there's absolutely nothing wrong with that! We just have to discern the difference between God's way of experiencing our two deepest desires and all the wrong ways of experiencing them.

If you think about it, **everything** we do in life boils down to these two words: pain and pleasure.

We are either trying to alleviate some sort of pain and/or obtain some sort of pleasure.

If you think about it this way: every *good* thing we do is to alleviate pain or obtain pleasure, and every *bad* thing we do is for the same two reasons!

We work to have the pleasure of comfort, peace of mind that our bills are paid, and the idea of a successful retirement that will make us happy. (And keep us insured, in case we get sick, right?!!!)

And if we steal or cheat, it's because we want to feel the pleasure of having the thing we don't think we can afford.

If we lie, we are trying to avoid the pain that the truth might bring. And so on . . .

If we lead someone to Jesus Christ, we are seeking the pleasure of knowing they'll be saved or alleviating the pain that Hell would bring and the misery of a life without God.

A child riding a merry-go-round, a jet pilot breaking the speed of sound, a tourist by a seashore, or a business person building a plan for a financial empire—all are searching for happiness.

Do you see? Everything falls into one of those two categories.

Even the most spiritual person who seeks only God and His highest glory, is made happy by the belief that God is honored.

Unhappiness and pain are such close cousins. Unhappiness results in high rates of so many other forms of pain—heart disease, stroke & sleeping disorders, obesity, and stress—just to name a few. Individuals suffering from depression are more likely to be unemployed or suffering from broken relationships.

Recent studies show the use of Facebook makes people feel worse about themselves. Studies have found using Facebook can reduce young adults' sense of well-being and satisfaction with life. University of Michigan research revealed the more some people browsed, the worse they felt.

These are some of the reasons the focus of this book is on the cure to pain and unhappiness. Because if we can tap into the cure of these two primary forces in life, we will be well on our way into the perfect will of God! And while that's a process, the sooner we start, the better! And it starts with the presence of God.

"You make known to me the path of life; in your presence there is fullness of joy; at your right hand are pleasures forevermore". (Psalm 16:11)

IN THE GARDEN: THE CENTER OF JOY

Chapter Three

Happiness was not only God's idea, it is part of God's nature. It flows from Him. **The Garden of Eden was the CENTER of happiness & joy.**

And out of the ground the LORD God gave growth to every tree that is pleasing to the eye and good for food. And in the middle of the garden were the tree of life and the tree of the knowledge of good and evil. (Genesis 2:9)

Notice, God gave them EVERY tree pleasing to the eye and good for food. And in the middle was the tree of life, and the tree of the knowledge of good and evil.

The tree of life symbolized Jesus. In fact, He went to the tree of death, because of Adam's sin; so that we could once again eat freely from the tree of life.

But when Adam & Eve first sinned, they unleashed the cursed DNA into the earth that began to spread. They unleashed every form of sorrow, sickness, disease, mental disorder, emotion disorder, lack, poverty, envy, hatred, depression, fear, sadness, and shame.

*" . . . in **sorrow** you shall bring forth . . . "* (Genesis 3:16)

*"Cursed is the ground because of you; through **painful** toil you will eat food from it all the days of your life."* (Genesis 3:17)

So, the curse that came upon mankind, when they sinned, began with unhappiness and pain.

An unhappy life. A painful existence. An unhappy birth and an unhappy death.

Notice what caused this downward spiral of unhappiness and pain:

- **They stopped believing what God said in Genesis 3:1, *"Hath God said?"*** Doubt led to the negative emotions of a sense of loss, that led to their downfall. *"God's holding out on you"*, was the devil's accusation. He got them to feel a sense of loss when they hadn't lost anything yet. But that sense of loss caused grief, sadness, and depression. This led them to their fateful decision.

- **They started blaming each other.** (Genesis 3:15) (That sure has continued ever since!)

- **Condemnation set in.** They knew they were naked. They were ashamed, they were afraid, and they felt guilty.

- **They started living** *"by the sweat of their brow"*, **immediately after they were separated from God.** (Genesis 3:19).

INDEPENDENCE FROM GOD produces profound unhappiness. Outside of His presence and grace, man is constantly striving to survive and get his needs met; and is chasing the things he lacks.

Don't be ashamed of the UNHAPPINESS or PAIN!

It's not a sin to feel sadness or pain. But Adam & Eve's false sense of loss and grief moved them to make emotionally-based decisions, which ruined their lives and the world.

Notice (and we're jumping ahead just enough to give the answer, but we have so much to fill in still) and contrast: their sadness and grief, leading to their decision to sin and curse the world forever to that with Jesus' moments of sadness and grief . . .

"And He took with Him Peter and James and John, and began to be struck with terror and amazement and deeply troubled and depressed. And He said to them, My soul is exceedingly sad (overwhelmed with grief) so that it almost kills Me! Remain here and keep awake and be watching." (Mark 14:33–34, AMPC)

Here Jesus began to reverse the curse! He felt the grief that mankind felt: grief, sorrow, and sadness—He felt all those things, but didn't sin. He took our pain, but didn't complain. So it's not a sin to feel those things. But Adam let those feelings lead to the deadly decision to eat from the tree he shouldn't.

Jesus didn't let His feelings control Him.

It says, *"And He went forward a little, and fell to the ground and prayed . . . "* (Mark 14:35).

He took His emotions to God in prayer, and by doing so, refused to be an emotionally-ruled Man. He then went to the cross and became the Tree of Life for all of us! Your healing begins as you believe that, and begin to expect His healing and joy to become a regular part of your life. As we believe in the finished work of the cross and fix our mind on these things, He will keep us in perfect peace. "Shalom" = peace, wholeness, happiness, and health. (Isaiah 26:3)

– The Cure: The Antidote to All Pain and Unhappiness

GOOD NEWS BRINGS GREAT JOY!

Chapter Four

Your breakthrough to healing and joy begin at Jesus' first entrance into this world. It's at His birth where unhappiness and pain began to finally meet their match! As soon as Jesus came to this earth, the verdict was in—*"Sin, sorrow, pain, unhappiness: your rule over mankind is coming to an end!"*

And everywhere He went, He brought joy and healing. In His presence is fullness of joy. *"And His presence melts the mountains of pain like wax!"* (Psalm 97:5)

So when Jesus comes to the earth, *"He is God with us"*. (Matthew 1:23) And His healing—joy-producing presence—is restored to the earth.

The world was a miserable place before Jesus was born. It was full of darkness and sin, even though it was full of religion and rules.

Religion makes men miserable, but God's grace makes men glad.

And the gospel of grace, which is the only gospel, is what brings healing and joy. We are saved by the grace that comes through the death, burial, and resurrection of Jesus Christ, not by any other thing. Notice the first people who were introduced to this grace, and the common result of their experience.

The Shepherds: *"And the angel said to them, 'Fear not: for, behold, I bring you good tidings of **great joy**: which shall be to all people'."* (Luke 2:9–10)

The Oxford dictionary simply describes joy as meaning, *"a feeling of great pleasure and happiness."*

Zacharias: Here, the angel Gabriel tells Zacharias of the son he would have in his old age, ***"You will have joy and gladness. And many will rejoice at His birth.*** For he will be great in the sight of the Lord . . ."* (Luke 1:14–15)

Mary: *"And Mary said: 'My soul exalts the Lord, And **my spirit has rejoiced in God** my Savior'."* (Luke 1:46–47) The word for "rejoice" here in verse 47, is the word, *agallia: a state of great joy and gladness.* The happiness of her soul was caused by what God had done for her.

The Magi: *"When they heard the king, they departed; and behold, the star which they had seen in the East went before them, till it came and stood over where the young Child was. When they saw the star, they rejoiced with **exceeding great joy.**"* (Matthew 2:9–10)

Why were they all so happy?

Because of the good news of Jesus' arrival!

The arrival of Jesus brings joy because it means: Your struggle is OVER! What struggle? The struggle to be loved; to be accepted; to beat the enemy; to move mountains; to get our faith to work; to see the promises of God; to live HOLY and godly. The grace that Jesus *is* and *brings* puts an end to our struggle for these things. He becomes all of these things for us!

"Behold, the virgin shall conceive and bear a son, and they shall call his name Immanuel" which means, God with us." (Matthew 1:23)

I'm so glad God didn't give Jesus the name, "God watching us" or "God judging us" or "God kind of near us." With the religion and belief I grew up with, God was distant, far from my everyday life. But the truth is: God's not out there some-where. (Well He is "there"; He is "here"; and all at the same time.) When you're going through your darkest moment, God is with you; and in your brightest day, He is the light. He is with you always. His presence makes the difference in our lives. He intends to walk with us, for us to feel He's with us all the time.

He is with us. The word "God" means: the Creator and the Father of Humanity. "With"—means: in our midst. "Us"—we are not alone.

THIS AWARENESS OF HIS PRESENCE BRINGS US JOY AND HAPPINESS.

RIGHT THINKING = RIGHT FEELING = RIGHT LIVING

Chapter Five

Studies show: 75% to 95% of the illnesses that plague us today are a direct result of our thought life. What we think about affects us physically and emotionally. It's an epidemic of toxic emotions.

"As a man thinks, so is he." (Proverbs 23:7)

The average person has over 30,000 thoughts a day. Through an uncontrolled thought life, we create the conditions for stress and illness; we make ourselves sick! Research shows that fear, all on its own, triggers more than 1,400 known physical and chemical responses and activates more than 30 different hormones. There are INTELLECTUAL and MEDICAL reasons to get our thinking straight regarding OURSELVES.

The overwhelming number of thoughts we have are negative. This is why we must renew our mind to God's way of thinking. There is nothing negative about Him. He is positively for you. He is positively on your side. He is positively with you. He is positively going to bring His promises to pass in your life. Believe that today!

But have you ever wondered what causes those moments or seasons of unhappiness? If we knew what God said about our situations, it would turn our sorrow into joy.

"These things I have spoken, that My joy might be in you and that your joy might be full!" (John 15:11)

God's **words** make us happy! So what are some of the *words* and *ways of thinking* that contribute to unhappiness or a joyless life?

Bad news: I also call this wrong information. The gospel is GOOD NEWS. We've been listening to the bad news—the wrong news. You are not defeated, trying to get the victory. You HAVE the victory, and you're trying to renew your mind to this truth.

You are NOW the head and not the tail.

We are NOW more than conquerors through Him that loved us.

God is NOW taking whatever bad has happened, and He's turning it into something good. (Romans 8:28)

Our path is getting brighter and brighter. (Proverbs 4:18) Listen to this GOOD NEWS and it will create a new pathway of pleasure in your thinking and in your life.

Bad memories: One of the things that keep us in pain or sorrow is our memory. We remember the hurt, the pain, and the mistakes we've made. We remember what others have done to us. We beat ourselves up about our past, and rehearse it and rehearse it; resulting in us imprisoning ourselves to the mental and emotional effects of our memories. Bad memories create a pathway to pain in our brains, while good memories create a pathway to pleasure. That's why there is so much in the Bible about remembering what God has done. *"Forget none of His benefits!"* (Psalm 103:1–5) According to Hebrews 10:17, in this covenant of grace, God treats His people as if they had never sinned.

It's forgotten now that the sacrifice of Jesus has ratified the covenant. We can rejoice in Him without fear that He will judge us or be angry with us. He makes us His children. He makes us righteous; He sees us as if we were perfectly holy. (Ephesians 4:24) He even puts us into places of influence; and makes us guardians of His galaxy! He makes us stewards of the greatest jewel of the universe: the gospel of Jesus Christ. The fact that He does all this is the highest evidence that He does not remember our sins. We are often slow to forgive an offense against us. But the Lord forgets our sins and treats us as if it had never been—Wow! Believe that. And you'll be happy.

Bad focus: We are focused on what we don't have. This is what makes us feel bad about our lives. We have to stop feeling bad about our lives.

Satan is doing a good job at getting people focused on what they don't have, and what they've done wrong—trying to limit us to become less than what we were born for—and that weighs our hearts down.

Begin today to appreciate what you have.

A University of California study done on successful people who found their secret to happiness. It found that 1 of their top 3 common characteristics was: **They appreciate what they have.**

They found that taking time to focus on what you're grateful for wasn't merely the *"right"* thing to do. They found it improved people's moods, because it reduced the stress hormone, cortisol, by 23%. The research found that people who worked daily to cultivate an attitude of gratitude experienced improved mood, energy, and physical well-being.

Ten lepers were cleansed, but only one returned to give God thanks.

"Then one of them, when he saw that he was healed, turned back, praising God with a loud voice; and he fell on his face at Jesus' feet, giving him thanks. Now he was a Samaritan. Then Jesus answered, "Were not ten cleansed? Where are the nine? Was no one found to return and give praise to God except this foreigner?" And he said to him, "Rise and go your way; your faith has made you whole." (Luke 17:15–19)

Notice, his giving of thanks seemed to cause his health to improve even more. Thankfulness made him whole!

– The Cure: The Antidote to All Pain and Unhappiness

THE SIX FIX!

Chapter Six

Let me list for you six simple things that will immediately increase your happiness, and begin to go to work on alleviating pain.

Charles Spurgeon, one of the greatest preachers of all time, argued that *"one is compelled to be happy simply by knowing that one's sins are forgiven"*. And he had sound biblical reasoning for believing so!

1. **"Happy is the man who knows his sins are forgiven."** Paul said this, quoting David in Romans 4:8.

I love what the NLT version says: *"Yes, what joy for those whose record the LORD has cleared of sin."*

Believe that you are forever forgiven in Christ. It is done!

2. **The supreme happiness in life is the assurance that we are loved.** God's divine love for us is the single most vital source of true happiness.

"As the Father has loved me, so have I loved you. Abide in my love . . . These things I have spoken to you, that my joy may

be in you, and that your joy may be full." (John 15: 9, 11) Notice, it is God's love for us that Jesus is speaking of. And He's saying that our understanding of that love will make our joy full!

3. *"Happy is he who does not condemn himself."* (Romans 14:22) Since there is no condemnation for those who are in Christ, the more we identify with our new creation reality—who we are in Christ—the happier we become. And when you've blown it, realize His mercy is new EVERY morning (Lamentations 3:22–23), and God will finish what He started in your life (Philippians 1:6).

4. **Happiness comes from trusting God.** *"O taste and see that the Lord is good. How happy is the man who trusts in Him!"* (Psalm 34:8–9, NLT)

Trust is simply believing God no matter what it looks or feels like. And it means trusting *God's faithfulness* to keep His promises rather than our faithfulness to earn His promises.

A promise to a child of a bicycle for Christmas is not a challenge to him to do his best to earn a bike by December 25th! It's an announcement of what the parents plan to do for him without his help.

5. **Refuse to accept that anyone has the power to make or break your happiness.** When we depend on someone else to make us happy, we give them control of our emotions. We must take control of our own emotions or they will take control over us. (Genesis 4:6–7)

6. **True happiness comes from true connection.** When we are connected with God, we are satisfied. Nothing else will satisfy us completely, the way intimacy with God does. (Song of Solomon 1:7, Song of Solomon 3:4)

– The Cure: The Antidote to All Pain and Unhappiness

JESUS IS OUR HEALER

Chapter Seven

*"Jesus went throughout Galilee, teaching in their synagogues, preaching the good news of the kingdom, and **healing EVERY disease and sickness among the people.** News about him spread all over Syria, and people brought to him **ALL** who were ill with various diseases, those suffering severe pain, the demon-possessed, those having seizures, and the paralyzed, and **He healed them.**"* (Matthew 4:23–24)

"BUT Jesus healed them all." (Matthew 4:24, CEV)

Look at our world today. Go online or turn on the TV and you'll see that; in every corner of the globe, there is an overflow of pain and suffering—enough to break your heart. Millions suffer from debilitating sickness and disease. A billion people have no access to clean drinking water, while 2 million people die each year (90% of them children) from waterborne diseases. 1 million children die each year of premature birth, while more than 15 million kids have been orphaned by AIDS. The world is filled with incidents of terrorism, violence, abuse, kidnappings, the horrors of war, heartbreak, and misery.

Sickness and disease is crippling families, economies, and destinies. Whether it's emotional or physical, heart disease or heartbreak, strokes or struggles, cancer or condemnation, respiratory & pulmonary disorders or depression & loneliness, people are in pain. No wonder Jesus came to heal!

In our church and in so many others, the number one prayer request is for healing for some sort of pain. Bodies are hurting. People are grieving. Some are suffering financially. Others are unhappy in their marriages, worried about their children, or wrestling with temptation or addiction.

So, yes, **pain is universal. It's part of the human condition—and always has been.**

Nowadays, the most popular solution to relieving pain is picking up a prescription for it. **3 out of 5 American adults are taking prescription medicine of some kind right now.**

There are over 120 *million* prescriptions written each year for antidepressants. I believe there is nothing wrong with taking medication under the supervision of a qualified medical professional (this is a part of God's merciful gifts of healing). And no one should feel condemned for using medical help. All healing is God's idea. BUT, things have gotten way out of hand. Antidepressant use has skyrocketed 65 percent in the last 15 years. And that's just for treating *emotional* pain. One study showed recently that **preschoolers** lead growth in antidepressant use. Over the last several years, it has gone up more than 50% among children 5 and under.

At the time of this writing, 115 people in America die each day from opioid or heroin overdose. That's one person every 11 or 12 minutes.

Overdose death rate for illicitly-obtained opioids like fentanyl— the drug involved in the death of *Prince*— is skyrocketing. It jumped 73% just from 2014 to 2015.

With that said, it's time to claim our rights as the children of God! *Healing is the children's bread*, Jesus said, in Matthew 15:26. And if you belong to Christ, you are one of the children that has the right to His healing!

SO, I want to share 5 things about healing today. As you grab a hold of these, healing will begin to flow from within your re-created spirit, into every area of your life.

1. **No one wants to keep hurting.** If they did, they'd never go to the doctor. They'd never take medicine. We know in our "knower" that we're not supposed to remain in pain. We seek to alleviate it. That's why half the advertisement in this world is for some sort of pain relief or release.

Yet, so often, people try to deal with their suffering without God, even though we weren't designed that way. Whether it's turning to substances, sexual sin, overeating, smoking, gambling, etc., these are ways people try to temporarily numb the pain.

God wants to be our Healer, and it's only He that truly is. He is Jehovah Rapha—the God who heals. He wants to be the One we look to. God says, *" . . . I am the Lord that heals you."* (Exodus 15:26).

2. **Jesus heals because Jesus loves.** Healing is a merciful act of God towards the sick and suffering. It has nothing to do with what we deserve.

"And Jesus went forth, and saw a great multitude, and was moved with compassion toward them, and he healed their sick." (Matthew 14:14)

In Jesus, we see that He chose to have compassion and mercy upon ANYONE who asked for it. Here are just a few examples:

Two Blind Men: *"As Jesus went on from there, two blind men followed him, crying loudly, 'Have mercy on us, Son of David'!"* (Matthew 9:27, NRSV)

Demon-Possessed Child: *"Just then a Canaanite woman from that region came out and started shouting, 'Have mercy on me, Lord, Son of David; my daughter is tormented by a demon'."* (Matthew 15:22, NRSV)

Epileptic Son: " . . . 'Lord, have mercy on my son, for he is an epileptic and he suffers terribly; he often falls into the fire and often into the water'." (Matthew 17:15, NRSV)

Another Two Blind Men: *"There were two blind men sitting by the roadside. When they heard that Jesus was passing by, they shouted, 'Lord, have mercy on us, Son of David!' The crowd sternly ordered them to be quiet; but they shouted* even more loudly, *'Have mercy on us, Lord, Son of David!'"* (Matthew 20:30, NRSV)

Gaderene Demoniac: *"But Jesus said to him, 'Go home to your friends, and tell them how much the Lord has done for you, and what mercy he has shown you'."* (Mark 5:19, NRSV)

Blind Bartimeus: *"When he heard that it was Jesus of Nazareth, he began to shout out and say, 'Jesus, Son of David, have mercy on me!' Many sternly ordered him to be quiet, but he cried out even more loudly, 'Son of David, have mercy on me'!"* (Mark 10:47, NRSV)

Ten Lepers: " . . . they called out, saying, *'Jesus, Master, have mercy on us'!"* (Luke 17:13, NRSV)

And He healed each and every one of them!

In the Old Testament, the Hebrew term for "mercy" is *chesed.* It is a magnificent word, often translated "lovingkindness" or God's loyalty to His covenant. It is His lovingkindness—His covenant love—His Blood-sworn oath—that moves Him to show mercy and love, no matter what.

3. **<u>Healing is God's will.</u>** *"Jesus went through all the towns and villages, teaching in their synagogues, preaching the good news of the kingdom and **healing EVERY disease and sickness."** (Matthew. 9:35)*

"And all the people were trying to touch Him, for power was coming from Him and healing them all." (Luke 6:19)

If He was healing **EVERY** disease and sickness, that must mean that He viewed sicknesses and diseases as a work of the enemy. And we also know that it was for this reason that He came—to destroy the works of the devil. (1 John 3:8)

Isn't it interesting that **NOWHERE** in the Bible did Jesus "sick" a healed person! But He sure healed the sick ones!

And nowhere did He say:

- **"This sickness is my gift to you."**

- **"This sickness is going to kill you, because I can't wait to see ya!"**

- **"Sorry kids, the healing store is closed. Come back . . . NEVER."**

- **"This sickness has been sent to make you more humble and to make you trust God more."**

- **"This disease is a way of teaching you to get your act together!"**

- **"It's just not My will"** (The ONLY time this issue was addressed in regards to Jesus and healing was the following: *"A man with leprosy came to him and begged him on his knees, 'If you are willing, you can make me clean'. Filled with compassion, Jesus reached out his hand and touched the man. **"I am willing"**, He said. 'Be clean'!"* (Mark 1:40–41). Notice God's final answer to whether it was His will: I AM WILLING. BE HEALED!

- **"You just don't have enough faith to receive your healing"** (Lazarus didn't have any faith. He was dead!)

If you hear someone using these excuses for things not happening, you are listening to man's religion, not the Gospel.

Jesus healed them and set them free from their oppressions. He never made excuses for sickness and disease to be there. He always recognized them as enemies to be conquered.

"When evening came, many who were demon-possessed were brought to him, and he drove out the spirits with a word and healed ALL the sick." (Matthew 8:16)

Again, if SOME sickness and disease was from God, He would not have been healing EVERY sickness and disease, because His Kingdom would then be divided against itself.

"As many as touched Him, WHEREVER HE WENT, were healed." (Mark 6:56)

*" . . . the crowds learned about it and followed him. He welcomed them and spoke to them about the kingdom of God, and **healed those who needed healing."** (Luke 9:11)

It doesn't say, *"He healed those who had no sin in their lives, or those who didn't have any generational curses, or people who didn't have unforgiveness in their hearts . . ."* He healed them all!

4. **Jesus paid for our healing on the cross.** *"But he was wounded for our transgressions, he was bruised for our iniquities: the chastisement of our peace was upon him; and with his stripes we are healed."* (Isaiah 53:5) *"He Himself bore our sins in His body on the cross, so that*

we might die to sin and live to righteousness. By His stripes you were healed." (1 Peter 2:24)

WE HAVE A COVENANT OF HEALING

A covenant is a solemn agreement between two parties. In this solemn agreement, the two parties dedicate themselves to granting at all times protection, promotion, and prosperity to each other

Real covenants are blood covenants. Covenants are ratified in blood. Covenants, in ancient and tribal societies, are made in blood.

The New Covenant had to be ratified in blood. Jesus, our High Priest, had to shed His own blood so that the NEW Covenant could go into effect.

Jesus made this plain on the night of His betrayal when, after eating the Passover meal with His disciples, He took the cup and said,

"This cup is the new covenant (ratified and established) in My blood." (Luke 22:20)

"He (Jesus Christ) is the mediator of a better covenant, which was established upon better promises." (Hebrews 8:6)

"If we belong to Christ, we are Abraham's seed, and heirs of the promise." (Galatians 3:29)

Remember the woman in Luke 13:10–16? She was bent doubled over for 18 years. Jesus said that satan had bound her. But JESUS said, *"Woman, thou art loosed!"* (Or was that TD Jakes who said that? Hahaha!) When they questioned Him, He said: *"This woman, being a daughter of Abraham, has the right to be healed today"!* AND SO DO YOU!

5. **All we need to do is receive.** WE CAN RECEIVE by believing it, speaking it, having hands laid on us, being anointed with oil, and even nutrition & medicine. These are all ways to receive the gift of healing.

The variety of ways don't contradict each other. They just confirm the abundant and over-the-top manifold GOODNESS OF GOD!

One of the ways I have found activates healing, time and time again, is through the celebration of communion. I believe when faith is released, miracles of healing can take place at the communion table. That's what happened to Cindy.

After years of suffering from migraines and epilepsy, Cindy heard me teaching about communion on TV, and she decided enough was enough. So she wrote me : *"After listening to your teaching on communion, the exercise of eating the bread and drinking the wine became more than just a ritual: it became an encounter with God. I literally felt a physical sensation in my head. As strange as it sounds, it was as though my brain was being warmly massaged, and immediately, I knew I had been touched by the Lord. I was healed! Since that time, the migraines are gone, the seizures are gone, and my epilepsy medication is gone."*

How awesome is that?!!!

And if you don't have a story like that, don't worry about it. Use this story, and the ones in scripture, as a prophetic picture of what's coming your way. Remember, the testimony of Jesus and what He has done in someone else's life, is the spirit of prophecy, and is an example of what He can do in yours! See Revelation 19:10.

THE NUMBER 1 CURE
FOR PAIN AND UNHAPPINESS

Chapter Eight

The moment I hope you've been reading for and waiting for . . . here is where both unhappiness and pain simultaneously meet their match!

Throughout scripture and throughout history, this one cure has been applied again and again, with astounding results. When received and given, it works miracles, physically, mentally, emotionally, and relationally as well!

What is it? You guessed it: FORGIVENESS.

Now whenever a preacher mentions the word 'forgiveness', our knee jerk reaction is to feel bad about maybe holding something against someone or preparing ourselves mentally to muster up the strength to forgive someone.

But that's NOT what I'm talking about.

I'm talking about *receiving* forgiveness.

And while forgiving others is powerful, you don't need any strength to do so.

Forgiving others is a REFLEX.

What do I mean by that? Well, forgiving others is an over-flow of receiving God's forgiveness for ourselves. You can't give what you don't have.

Under the old covenant, we had to forgive others, in order to be forgiven. Jesus was teaching Jewish people under the law that FIRST they had to forgive and THEN they could be forgiven.

"But if you do not forgive, neither will your Father who is in heaven forgive your transgressions." (Mark 11:26)

But the New Covenant reverses that. Yes, I know v.26 says to give it first and then receive it. BUT, Jesus taught that BEFORE His blood was shed. His teaching was done, as were His works, as a fulfillment of the Law. He said, *"I didn't come to destroy the law, but fulfill it."*

I don't want to go too far down this rabbit trail, but suffice it to say: the New Covenant didn't start with Jesus' teachings; it started with the shedding of His blood!

"This cup is the blood of my New Covenant . . . " (Matthew 26:28)

A covenant does not go into effect until the death of the one who makes it. (Hebrews 9:17)

My point in all of that, is to circle back to forgiveness and reinforce that the New Covenant reverses the order of how to experience it.

"Forbearing one another, and forgiving one another, if any man have a quarrel against any: even as Christ forgave you, so do also." (Colossians 3:13)

Notice the emphasis: forgive one another . . . EVEN AS CHRIST FORGAVE YOU, so do also.

- **He forgave you.** It's written in the past tense. It's already done.

- **EVEN AS He forgave you,** means that forgiving others, CAN ONLY come after receiving it ourselves.

Do you see the difference? Under the old covenant, forgiveness had to be given BEFORE being received. (This wasn't completely possible or practical, but it forced man to realize His need for a Savior!) But under the New Covenant, forgiveness HAS to be RECEIVED before it can be given. And thankfully, Jesus has already forgiven you. All you have to do is believe it.

When you do, it becomes a reflex to believe that others are forgiven freely by His grace, just as you have been. And that results in you releasing them, from what you know you have been released from already—all your sins, blunders, and mistakes!

THE 7 MIRACLES
OF FORGIVENESS

Chapter Nine

Now here I want to show you 7 miracles of receiving and giving forgiveness.

1. Forgiveness is THE SECRET TO HAPPINESS.

As we shared in an earlier chapter, forgiveness really is a gateway to happiness. There is a neurological path in our brain that leads to what is called: the pleasure center of the brain. That path is blocked by holding our own sins against ourselves or someone else's.

If you can imagine a super clear highway to the destination of your dreams, that is what it looks like in your brain. The path to "the pleasure center" is always there, but it's blocked and full of bumper to bumper traffic! Forgiveness opens the highway and brings you to that destination.

I hope you grab a hold of this merging of the gospel and science or physiology. When this path is blocked through hating ourselves, holding something against ourselves, or offenses and bitterness, WE PUMP other things into the highway to widen it and reach the pleasure center. That's why people take other substances or commit other addictive behaviors, to bypass the proper pathway, in an attempt to reach the pleasure center. We crave pleasure and if the pathway is blocked, we force something in that will open it up; when what's really needed is: having mercy on yourself and others through the blood of Jesus; joy and peace will flow like a river!

"Happy is he whose transgression is forgiven, whose sin is pardoned." (Psalm 32:1)

"Blessed, how joyful, how happy . . . " (Romans 4:7, JPS)

*"Yes, what joy for those whose **record the LORD has cleared of sin.**"* (Romans 4:8, NLT)

Charles Wesley, in his wonderful hymn, reminded us of that: He breaks the power of canceled sin and sets the captive free. His blood can make the foulest clean; His blood availed for me.

2. **Forgiveness LEADS TO YOUR INHERITANCE and blessing.**

" . . . *That they may receive forgiveness, AND THEIR INHERITANCE."* (Acts 26:18) Notice, first comes receiving forgiveness, which leads to being able to receive the rest of your inheritance in Christ. That inheritance includes the blessing of Abraham and all the blessings of Deuteronomy 28, without the curses—because Jesus redeemed us from the curse, but didn't redeem us from the blessing. He paid for us to have the blessings! (Galatians 3:13–14)

3. **Forgiveness IS THE SECRET TO HEALING.**

In Mark 2, the friends of a sick man brought him to Jesus. You know the story. When they couldn't' find a way in the house, they lowered him through the roof. When Jesus saw the young man, he said, *"Son, your sins are forgiven."*

He came for healing, but Jesus gave him forgiveness. THEN Jesus healed him. There are a number of reasons Jesus forgave him first. But the focus for us is that He was showing us the pathway to healing—receiving God's forgiveness. He's showing us that FREELY receiving forgiveness opens the door to receive healing in the same way: freely. When we realize we are forgiven freely, (even though we still may stumble or fall, we are still ALREADY FORGIVEN), we can learn to receive all God's gifts freely—though we haven't earned them and can't earn them. They are gifts.

4. **Forgiveness EXPOSES THE DEVIL & SPOILS HIS PLOT AGAINST YOU.**

"Now to whomever you forgive anything, I also forgive; for indeed if I have forgiven anything, it is for your sake, in the presence of Christ, in order that we may not give Satan an advantage (or an inroad); for we are not ignorant of his schemes and devices." (2 Corinthians 2:10, 11)

Paul is saying here that the reason he forgives someone is through the presence of Christ (through his blood), because unforgiveness gives satan an advantage and an inroad. And we must not remain ignorant of this roadway the enemy uses to mess with our lives. Forgiveness shuts the door to demonic activity in our lives. Wow!

5. **Receiving forgiveness causes you to love supernaturally!**

" . . . she has been forgiven much, therefore she loves much. But to whom little is forgiven, they love little." (Luke 7:47)

This is a powerful truth, because again, it shows the reflex of forgiveness. It causes love to flow. We don't need more love. It's been shed abroad in our hearts by the Holy Spirit. We need more love *to flow*. And what causes it to flow is to know how much we have been forgiven. That revelation makes you generous in your love and with everything else in your life.

It also creates better and freer relationships in every way, every day!

6. **Forgiveness lowers risk of substance abuse: alcohol, drugs, and pornography, etc.**

This is a big one. I feel this is one of the biggest and best reasons to jump into a forgiveness practice like, um, yesterday! Substance abuse is a mask for underlying pain. Forgiveness helps us release that pain and find something good in our situation instead. Forgiveness reduces stress and the chemicals in our brain that cause us to crave substances.

It cures & STRENGTHENS YOUR IMMUNE SYSTEM. See Ephesians 4:26. In a study done at Virginia Commonwealth University, researchers found what we might already know as common sense. They wrote, *"Chronic unforgiveness causes* stress. *Every time people think of their transgressor, their body responds. Decreasing your unforgiveness cuts down your health risk. Now, if you can forgive, that can actually strengthen your immune system."*

It produces emotional healing too. **Doctor Karl Menninger,** one of the world's most successful medical doctor & psychiatrists, did a study of the cure for mental illness; and at the end of his study, he said, *"I can take any patient who's mentally ill and I can rid them of at least 75 percent of all their mental illness with one word—forgive."*

Dr. Bernie Siegel, well-known writer, surgeon, and retired medical professor at Yale University, stated, *"I have collected 57 extremely well-documented so-called cancer miracles. At a certain particular moment in time, they decided that the anger and the depression were probably not the best way to go, since they had such little time left.*

And so they went from that to being loving, caring, no longer angry, no longer depressed, and able to talk to the people they loved. ***These 57 people had the same pattern.*** *They gave up—totally—their anger, and they gave up—totally—their* *depression, by specifically a decision to do so. And at that point the tumors started to shrink."*

7. FORGIVENESS LEADS TO PROMOTION AND PURPOSE.

In Genesis 37:24, Joseph's brothers *"took him and threw him into a pit. Now the pit was empty, without any water in it."*

Then in Genesis 37:28, *"they pulled him up and lifted Joseph out of the pit, and sold him to the Ishmaelites for twenty shekels of silver. Thus they brought Joseph into Egypt."*

Then in Genesis 39:1, *"Now Joseph had been brought down to Egypt, and Potiphar, an officer of Pharaoh, the captain of the guard, an Egyptian, had bought him from the Ishmaelites, who had brought him down there."* **Verse 2 says, "BUT THE LORD WAS WITH HIM."** (Romans 8:31 says. *"If God be for you, who can be against you."*)

Acts 7:9 puts it this way: *"And the patriarchs, having envied Joseph, sold him into Egypt. But God was with him."*

Now this short section is covering a lot of ground, but let's quickly jump to Genesis 45:4–5 after Joseph reveals

his identity to his brothers for the first time. *" . . . Then Joseph said to his brothers, 'Please come closer to me.' And they came closer. And he said, 'I am your brother Joseph, whom you sold into Egypt. Now do not be grieved or angry with yourselves because you sold me here; for God sent me before you, to preserve life'."*

Genesis 50:15 says, *"When Joseph's brothers saw that their father was dead, they said, 'What if Joseph bears a grudge against us and pays us back in full for all the wrong which we did to him'!"*

Genesis 50:19 says, *"Do not be afraid. Am I in the place of God?"* Who are we to hold something against someone that even God doesn't hold against them?

Verse 20 says, *"You meant evil. But God meant good."*

Don't forgive people because they didn't mean it. Forgive them because THEY MEANT IT.

The story of Joseph here is the epitome of a forgiving heart. It is undeniable proof that even if man decides to hurt you, even if man decides to rob you of your best part of life, nothing can ultimately prevail against what God has destined. And therefore, there is no need to hold a grudge against anyone. Because when you hold a grudge against people that hurt you, you're saying that person has more power than God. But when you realize that God's power is able to turn the situation around, there's no more purpose for holding unforgiveness. We hold unforgiveness because we think that person has control over us. We're mad at what they did, because we think that what they did will stop the best life that we want.

But it can't, unless we refuse to forgive.

Forgiveness FREES US FROM BEING CONTROLLED BY THE CHOICES OTHERS MAKE.

"Forbearing one another, and forgiving one another, if any man have a quarrel against any: even as Christ forgave you, so also do ye." (Colossians 3:13)

THE WORD: ONE ANOTHER—in Greek, *heautaus*, actually means: *HIMSELF, YOURSELF, and then reflexively, others.* It starts with ourselves here.

Forgive yourself. Love yourself.

You know, if you look in the mirror right now and look yourself in the eye, but you don't like the person that you're looking at, there's only one thing to do—forgive yourself. God made you to like yourself, but satan's accusing you and trying to convince you that the shape of your ears have to change before you can be happy—or you have to stop getting angry to be happy or change some habit in order to stop the guilt to be happy. And it's all a lie. What you need to do is realize that there's something in you that feels guilty about what you've done or shame about who you are. You either feel guilt or you feel shame and that's what's making you dislike yourself. It's not that you're not pretty enough or holy enough. Maybe you feel bad because you're comparing yourself to somebody else rather than looking at the person that God loves so much—He created you and died for you, so that He could have a relationship with YOU! And if the Prince of the universe and the King of kings and Lord of lords wants to be with you, that means you are beautiful, valuable, and amazing to Him. And He doesn't want to ever miss out on having an intimate relationship with you. So you know what? You need to let go of guilt and forgive yourself so that you can start loving yourself the way God loves you.

THIS IS SIMPLY CATCHING UP TO WHAT GOD HAS ALREADY DONE. He has already forgiven you.

When you believe this, everything is going to be alright! Healing and happiness will begin to flow like a river. And they will never stop!

DECISION & DECLARATION OF FORGIVENESS

Chapter Ten

Our choices and our words have power. Forgiveness starts with a decision, and is enforced with our words. Death and life are in the power of the tongue. As you read the declarations of forgiveness below, speak them aloud and expect the freedom Jesus paid for, to flow like a river in your life.

Decide and Declare: **I forgive** myself for failing or falling short; for the self-sabotage and self hatred I've allowed to happen. **I let go of feeling damaged, inadequate, and unworthy.**

I forgive myself for not being a better person or parent, spouse or Christian. I'm letting go of the guilt for the times I let others down.

I forgive myself for the selfish choices I've made that have hurt me and hurt others.

I forgive myself for not being the best version of myself and robbing people of the beauty of what that would have been. I give myself the gift of letting go of regret.

I forgive those who let me down. And I believe Jesus lifts me up. I am not a victim anymore.

I forgive my family members that have let me down with their anger, addiction, or selfishness. I'm letting go of the painful memories so I can better remember the times when they were just my family members.

I forgive the people who said they would be my friend, but then disappeared or disappointed. I'm letting go of the anger, so I can make room for new friendships.

I forgive those who have hurt me, taken advantage of me, thought poorly of me, or treated me as less valuable than God intended.

I give the gift of forgiveness to myself and others, freely, just as Jesus has given it freely to me!

Special Note: In each of my books, I desire to help lead people to the Lord—if they have never been born again, or are not certain of their salvation. Please use this for yourself or for someone you know who may not know the Lord yet.

THE GIFT OF SALVATION

Your New Life Begins
with God's Love

"This is the kind of love we are talking about—not that we once upon a time loved God—but that He loved us and sent His Son as a sacrifice to clear away our sins and the damage they've done to our relationship with God."

—1 John 4:10b MSG

Christianity is not a religion. It is a relationship between God and you.

God loves you deeply and wants a personal relationship with you! The Love of Jesus Christ will sweep away your sin, loneliness, pain, and fear. He wants you to spend eternity in Heaven with Him, and the rest of your life on this earth walking with Him. If you would like to begin a new life—beyond your wildest dreams and be born again—pray the following prayer, and believe in your heart that God answers!

"Heavenly Father, I believe that Jesus Christ died on the cross for my sins and rose from the dead. His blood washes away my past, my sins; and prepares me for eternity. I receive Your forgiveness and accept Jesus as my Savior and Lord. From this day forward, I am Yours, in Jesus' Name. Amen!"

If you have prayed this prayer, we would love to hear from you. Please call us at 847-645-9700, or simply email us at prayer@changinglives.org.

AS YOU
GO FORWARD

Next Steps

As a believer, I encourage you to step out in faith and live every day as if it were your first day living for God. I also encourage you to do the following three things:

1. Read your Bible. The Bible has the answer to every problem that you could ever face. As you read and study, know that you have the same promises that God gave Abraham, David, and all of the great men and women in the Bible. You will find out exactly who you are and what you mean to Him. You will find out that He will never leave you or forsake you! You will be filled with strength and wisdom.

2. Get planted in church. By now, you understand the power that comes from the church family. You don't need to go to church to get into heaven, but you **DO** need to become equipped to fulfill God's will for your life. In Luke 4:16, we find it was Jesus' custom to go to church every week. If the Son of God made it His custom, how much more should we?

3. Tell Somebody. One of the most rewarding things I have ever found in my life is the opportunity to share with others what God has done for me. You don't have to be a preacher. Just tell someone your simple story of God's love and plant the seed of the gospel in someone's life. You will be blessed, and so will they!

Well, what a journey you've just begun! And it is just that—a journey. Remember, the power of a new life is a process. It begins the moment you are born again, but it continues through our lives. We all face storms and trials, and we have an enemy, the devil, trying to stop our progress. But God has given us the tools and weapons to resist the enemy and be victorious in our journey. Build your life on these foundations and you will not fail!

"And the rain fell, and the floods came, and the winds blew and beat against that house; and yet it did not fall, for it had been founded on the rock." (Matthew 7:25)

Gregory Dickow Ministries &
Life Changers International Church Mission Statement

"Introducing people to the real Jesus;
empowering them to rise to their true worth
& purpose; and changing mind-sets
that change the world."

OTHER BOOKS AVAILABLE BY PASTOR GREGORY DICKOW

- Breaking the Power of Inferiority
- Fast From Wrong Thinking
- From the Inside Out
- How to Never be Hurt Again
- More Than Amazing Grace
- So Loved
- The Power to Change Today
- Thinking Forward
- Winning the Battle of the Mind

AUDIO SERIES AVAILABLE BY PASTOR GREGORY DICKOW

- Breaking the Power of Shame
- Command Your Day
- Fearless Living
- Healing the Father Fracture
- Identity
- Living in the State of Grace: Relocating to the Best Place on Earth
- Love Thyself
- Mastering Your Emotions
- Radical Acceptance
- The End of Religion
- The Holy Spirit, Our Healer
- Visions & Dreams

You can order these and many other life-changing materials by calling toll-free **1-888-438-5433**. For more information about Gregory Dickow Ministries, please visit **www.gregorydickow.com**.